D0465833

Contents

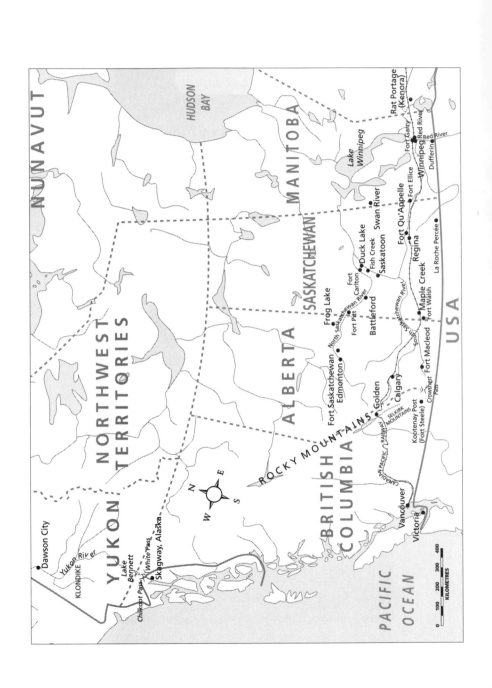

The Mounties

Tales of Adventure and Danger from the Early Days

by Elle Andra-Warner

For my daughter, Cindi

PUBLISHED BY ALTITUDE PUBLISHING CANADA LTD.
1500 Railway Avenue, Canmore, Alberta T1W 1P6
www.altitudepublishing.com
www.amazingstories.ca
1-800-957-6888

Based on a book with the same title
by Elle Andra-Warner, first published in 2004.

Extreme care has been taken to ensure that all information presented in
this book is accurate and up to date. Neither the author nor the
publisher can be held responsible for any errors.

Publisher	Stephen Hutchings
Associate Publisher	Kara Turner
Junior Edition Series Editor	Linda Aspen-Baxter
Editor	Lisa Lamb
Cover and Layout	Bryan Pezzi

We acknowledge the financial support of the Government
of Canada through the Book Publishing Industry Development
Program (BPIDP) for our publishing activities.

Altitude GreenTree Program
Altitude Publishing will plant twice as many trees as were used
in the manufacturing of this product.

ISBN 10: 1-55439-705-7
ISBN 13: 978-1-55439-705-1

Amazing Stories® is a registered trademark of Altitude Publishing Canada Ltd.

Printed and bound in Canada by Friesens
2 4 6 8 9 7 5 3 1

Prologue

For three days a raging blizzard had blown on Bathurst Island. Two Royal Canadian Mounted Police (RCMP) officers and their guide were forced to stay in their igloo. It was the winter of 1929. Inspector Joy and Constable Taggart were on an 81-day patrol. This patrol would take them 2700-kilometres through the Arctic's Parry Islands.

On the third night the men were sleeping inside their igloo. Suddenly, their sled dogs began to bark fiercely. Inspector Joy looked outside. He saw a huge polar bear in their camp. Usually the dogs would scare the polar bears away. Usually, but not on that night.

The polar bear approached the group's supply sled. He began to claw at the covering. Watching from the igloo, Joy asked the others for the rifle. It was then that the men realized they were sunk. Their only firearm was sitting outside the igloo. Quickly, the three men started to clear away the ice and snow blocking the entrance.

With their snow knives they slashed at the ice and snow. They frantically shouted out orders to each other. Their voices brought the curious bear to the igloo. The animal charged at the igloo.

Shouting and screaming, the men began to cut a different hole. They knew where their rifle was. They wanted to cut a hole by the rifle so they could reach it. The bear saw them. He lunged at that hole. The men had to fight back.

The guide slashed at the bear with his knife. Constable Taggart swung a club at the animal. He hit it hard on the tip of its nose. Snarling, the bear backed away. At that moment, Taggart tried to reach the rifle. The bear saw him. The bear attacked. Constable Taggart was forced back into the igloo.

Again Taggart hit the bear's nose. Again the bear drew back. The constable grabbed the rifle, but the bear lunged. It knocked the weapon from Taggart's hand. The gun fell to the icy ground. The polar bear stood on it. Helpless, Taggart rushed back into the igloo. There he joined his terrified partners.

Chapter 1
How It All Began

It was one of the greatest real estate deals of all time. On July 15, 1870, the Dominion of Canada finally owned all of Canada. It had paid £300,000 to the Hudson's Bay Company (HBC). The money bought the control of Rupert's Land.

Rupert's Land was a huge chunk of property. It was equal to almost 40 percent of modern-day Canada. This area included all of today's Manitoba, Saskatchewan, Alberta, Yukon, Northwest Territories, and Nunavut. It also included large parts of Quebec and Ontario.

The Hudson's Bay Company had ruled this area of land for more than 200 years. The Hudson's Bay Company received the land on May 2, 1670. They owned it through the Royal Charter. The Royal Charter was granted by England's king, Charles II.

The grant had given the HBC absolute powers over the land. This power included the right to create and enforce laws. The HBC could also have its own army and navy. They could make peace with the Native peoples. Or they could make war.

Rupert's Land had been named after Prince Rupert. Prince Rupert was the cousin of King Charles II. Rupert's Land stretched more than five million square kilometres. And now Canada owned it all.

There was one problem. Its prairies were wild and lawless. Some areas were very dangerous. It was land filled with warring Native tribes. Hunters hunted without care and dishonest traders roamed the land. They ignored the law. Many lived by the gun.

The American traders who crossed into Canada caused trouble. They traded guns and homemade whisky to the Native peoples. They took back buffalo robes and furs. The whisky was also known as "firewater." It was a wicked mixture of pure alcohol, water, tobacco juice, ginger, and molasses.

The Americans would trade one or two cupfuls of whisky for a buffalo hide. The liquor was destroying the Native peoples. The demand for buffalo hides was wiping out the buffalo herds.

These American whisky traders set up trading posts across the Prairies. Some forts were as far north as present-day Edmonton. Most of the forts were small and cabin-like. They would only be used for a season or two. These traders did as they pleased. They did not listen to laws of the Hudson's Bay Company.

The largest whisky trading post was Fort Whoop-Up. It was in the foothills of the Rocky Mountains, just south of present-day Lethbridge, Alberta. This trading post made a lot of money for the traders. Fort Whoop-Up belonged to Alfred Baker Hamilton, John Jerome Healy, and Healy's brother Thomas. All of them were from Fort Benton, Montana. Fort Benton was just across the border on the Missouri River.

The men of Fort Whoop-Up traded the wicked whisky to the Native peoples. There was nobody there to stop them. The whisky sold at Fort Whoop-Up was nicknamed "Whoop-Up Bug Juice." It was made of whisky, chewing tobacco, red pepper, Jamaica ginger, and molasses. Water was added to these ingredients. Then it was boiled. Whoop-Up Bug Juice was traded by the cupful or by the keg to the Native peoples. Many did not understand the dangers of this firewater. Many would get drunk. Often they would become violent. Sometimes there were killings outside the walls of the fort. One time, they burned down all 11 log huts of Fort Whoop-Up.

Besides whisky, there were other goods traded. The goods were brought into Canada by bull wagon. The goods included items like tobacco, guns, blankets, cloth, sugar, canned goods, and mirrors.

In 1870, after the fire, the American traders rebuilt the fort. This time they built it large and solid so that it could not be burned down again or attacked. A large, five-metre-tall oak gate was the entrance to the fort. Guns and cannons were positioned so that they could be fired at anyone who was not invited.

Inside the heavy log walls of the fort were rooms to live in and run a business from. There were storerooms, living quarters, a kitchen, a blacksmith shop, and stables. The roof was made of logs. The logs were covered with sod. This prevented Native peoples from setting the fort on fire by shooting flaming arrows. The chimneys were crossed with iron bars for protection.

Native peoples were not allowed inside this new fort. They traded through a small window. The Native peoples would push their buffalo robes through the window. The trader then handed them the tin cupfuls of whisky in return.

The Canadian government saw what was happening. They knew they would have to stop this type of trading. Whisky was terrible. It was affecting the lives of the Native peoples of the Prairies.

The Canadian government wanted to quickly settle the Canadian West. Homesteaders from Europe were being invited to come and farm the land. But the violence of the land was making it difficult. Also, the government was concerned that Americans might move onto the land and claim it as their own. They worried that the U.S. Cavalry might cross into Canada. If there were no police, no one could stop them.

Prime Minister Sir John A. Macdonald began planning. He needed to figure out how best to deliver law and order to the Canadian West. He liked the idea of a police force on horseback. He thought of the Royal Irish Constabulary (RIC) and India's Bengal Mounted Police.

On May 3, 1873, Macdonald introduced a bill to the Canadian Parliament. He introduced the idea of a force of mounted riflemen. He called them a "Police Force for the North-West Territories."

The North-West Territories was the name given to almost the whole Rupert's Land. The Territories covered all the area except the Red River settlement region. The Red River region became the province of Manitoba. It joined the Dominion of Canada in 1870.

The Canadian Parliament passed the bill for the new police force. Looking for the men to start this police force did not happen immediately. Then something happened. The Canadian West urgently needed a police force.

The Cypress Hills Massacre
The Cypress Hills Massacre began in late May 1873. Wolf hunters who used poisoned buffalo meat as bait were called wolfers. A group of wolfers left Fort Benton, Montana. They crossed into Canada. They came looking for some Cree men. They suspected the men of stealing some of their horses.

The group was out for revenge. They followed the stolen horse tracks to Cypress Hills. It was 60 kilometres north of the Canadian-American boundary (in today's southwestern Saskatchewan).

The area was a camping ground for Native peoples. It had also become a centre for whisky traders. American Abel Farwell and German-born Moses Solomon had built their trading posts — Farwell's Fort and Solomon's Post. The two posts were almost directly across from each other on the Milk River (now called Battle Creek).

Farwell, a tall, heavy man, was popular with the Native peoples in the area. He had married a Cree woman named Mary Horseguard. She worked alongside him as his partner. New Brunswick-born George Hammond also worked at Farwell's Fort.

The Benton wolfers dropped into Farwell's Fort for some drinking. There they heard that about 200 Assiniboine people were camped on a flat piece of prairie. They were camped along the Milk River. The wolfers shifted their anger with the Cree onto the nearby Native camp. They started making attack plans.

Farwell told the Benton gang that the Assiniboine people had not stolen their horses. He could see it didn't matter what he said. The wolfers wanted to kill. It is even said that the wolfers sent a keg of liquor to the Assiniboine people. This would get them drunk. Then it would be easier to kill them.

According to stories, Farwell tried to prevent the violence by going to meet with the Assiniboine leader, Little Soldier. While the two men were talking, the wolfers arrived. They called out for Farwell to get out of the way. Farwell shouted back. If they fired, he would fight with the Native peoples.

He asked the Benton wolfer gang to hold off. He wanted to go back to the fort to get his interpreter, Alexis LeBombard. Alexis LeBombard would try to settle the matter peacefully. As Farwell raced back to the post, the first shots rang out. The killing had begun.

Some stories claim that Little Soldier tried to wake up his warriors. But many were drunk. It was too late. The wolfers captured Little Soldier. They killed him. Then they cut off his head and mounted it on a long pole.

Next were the men, women, and children. They even shot and killed the elders who were hiding in the riverbeds. The Assiniboine could not stop the wolfers. Any survivors quickly scrambled to safety in the hills. Some found safety at a nearby Métis camp.

After the massacre at daybreak, the wolfers stole from the Assiniboine people. Then they set fire to the camp. It was a horrible sight. Dead bodies were scattered among the burning lodges. Little Soldier's head was still on a lodge pole high above the camp. More than 30 Assiniboine had been murdered. All of them had been innocent of horse theft.

Only one of the wolfers had died. Farwell and Solomon feared for their lives. They quickly loaded their wagons and left.

News of the Cypress Hills Massacre reached the

Canadian government in early September. The massacre pushed the government to bring the mounted police into the West quickly.

On September 25, 1873, nine officers were chosen to form the new force. They had to find 150 men and get them to Stone Fort. Stone Fort was also known as HBC's Lower Fort Garry. It was called Stone Fort by the Native peoples of the area. The name Stone Fort was used by the Mounties.

Mountie Politics

Posters were placed everywhere. The posters called for men who were:
- healthy,
- active and fit,
- able to ride a horse,
- of good character,
- able to read and write either the English or French language,
- and were between the ages of 18 and 40 years.

The job was for three years. After three years, each NWMP member would receive 160 acres of land in the North-West Territories. This offer was later taken away.

The force was divided into troops. Each troop was headed by a commissioner. The pay was terrible. Sub-constables earned 75 cents per day. Constables earned $1. Veterinary surgeons earned $400 to $600 per year. Superintendents and surgeons earned $1000 to $1400.

Commissioners earned $2000 to $2600 per year.

Despite the poor pay, joining the police was appealing. Those with a spirit and thirst for adventure applied for the job. One young recruit later wrote about joining the NWMP troop. He wrote that he thought life would be one grand adventure. He would ride wild mustangs. He would chase whisky traders and horse thieves. And he hoped he would meet lovely princesses.

The bill that was passed allowed 300 men to join the NWMP. The government felt 150 was enough. After all, there were not many people living in the West yet. Thousands of men applied. In September 1873, they flocked to centres in Ontario, Quebec, and the Maritimes. In Toronto alone there were 622 applicants for 50 vacancies.

The chosen men were divided into three troops. Each troop had 50 men. The troops were named Troops A, B, and C. Nine farmers, 46 clerks, 13 police or military men, 43 skilled workers, and 39 listed men with no previous experience were hired.

The first commissioner of the mounted police was Lieutenant Colonel George Arthur French. French was a gunner born in Roscommon, Ireland. He was later educated in the British military. He had come to Canada in 1871 as a military inspector. He was asked to come by the Canadian government. In Canada, he became the head of the School of Gunnery in Kingston. In 1873, French was appointed to organize the NWMP.

French worked until 1876. He then returned to duty in the British Army. He received a knighthood in 1902. For the next 19 years he guarded the crown jewels in London, England. French died in 1921.

The First Trek

In early October 1873, the men came together. They met at the Collingwood docks on Lake Huron. From Lake Huron they sailed 875 kilometres by steamboat to Prince Arthur's Landing. This was on the western shores of Lake Superior. Prince Arthur's Landing was renamed Port Arthur. It is now part of the city of Thunder Bay.

From Prince Arthur's Landing, they would travel almost 700 kilometres to Stone Fort. Stone Fort is south of today's Winnipeg. It was a hard and unpredictable route. The route took them through forests, lakes, rivers, and swamps.

Simon J. Dawson first surveyed the route in 1858. Ten years later, the government ordered him back. He was to build the route as a trail. Settlers headed west would travel along the trail. Named the Dawson Route, it was known as the only "all-Canadian" route to the North-West. It did, however, briefly dip three times into the United States.

In 1870, during the first Riel Rebellion, a Red River expedition used the trail. The group was led by Colonel John Garnet Wolseley. There were 1200 soldiers — both Canadian militia and British troops. They were sent to

Manitoba to restore order.

The group included future members of the police. Leaders like Sam Steele, James Walsh, and James Macleod made the trek. It was a brutal journey. It involved road building, navigating, poling, tracking, and tackling more than 40 difficult portages.

Now, three years later, Steele, Macleod, and Walsh would again trek on the difficult Dawson Route to Manitoba.

Arriving in the West

Troop A, led by 33-year-old Inspector James Walsh, left Collingwood first. On October 4, 1873, 41 men boarded the paddlewheel steamer *Cumberland*. Before the steamer left the dock, an order was given to the troops. They were not to drink too much. They could drink, but any drunkenness would be reported.

On October 10, the second group left. It was made up of 62 men and two officers. After a stormy passage on Lake Superior, Troop B arrived at Prince Arthur's Landing. It joined Troop A. Together they started down the Dawson Route. They travelled with three-horse wagons. They had excellent fall weather so made good travelling time. The two troops arrived at Stone Fort on October 22.

Troop C had 53 men. With officers Young, Brennan, and James Macleod, Troop C left Collingwood on October 10. Their steamer was named *Frances Smith*.

From the beginning, they were faced with terrible weather and bad luck.

The *Frances Smith* ran into a severe snowstorm on Lake Superior. It was reported that the crossing was one of the roughest in four years. Everyone got violently seasick, except for Inspector Macleod. After arriving at Prince Arthur's Landing, the group loaded up the wagons. They prepared to travel the remaining 600 kilometres to Stone Fort.

The Dawson Route had several "stopping houses." Travellers could stop and get a meal for 30 cents. They could also buy new supplies. Unfortunately, by the time this group set out on the trail, the stopping houses were empty. They had thought that all the NWMP troops had already travelled by. So they closed for the winter.

It was now late October. Winter was settling in. The men of Troop C would have to travel hundreds of kilometres without supplies or places to stop and eat. The next fort was the HBC's Fort Frances. It was located almost 300 kilometres away. The officers decided there would be no turning back. They would have to continue west and take their chances.

Along the route they broke into every stopping house. They were tired and hungry and tried to find food. Winter's snow came early. As they reached Rainy Lake, boats were there to meet them. The boats were piloted by Iroquois crews. They would take the men to Fort Frances. The Iroquois had no food for them.

The men were disappointed. But they were eager to arrive at Fort Frances. There they would finally be able to purchase food and supplies — or so they thought. The moment they landed, they went to the Hudson's Bay post. They asked for anything the store had for supper for 70 men. But there was nothing. There was only two barrels of cube sugar. There was no flour. There wasn't even an ounce of meat.

Saddened, the men spent the night on the snow-covered beach. All they had to wear was their summer clothes. They had no winter boots. None of them had warm coats or blankets. The only food for breakfast was the dried apples they had taken from a stopping house. Hungry and cold, the next day they ran the three-kilometre Meline Rapids. There they would reach Rainy River.

Their luck turned for a time. Nearby, they found a Chippewa camp. At the camp was a lot of white fish and corn. The Chippewa were readying their food for the winter. They stopped and made a large meal of boiled fish and corn for the starving NWMP.

After camping beside the Chippewa for the night, Troop C headed out the next morning. Terrible weather followed them again. As they reached the mouth of the Lake of the Woods, a violent snowstorm blew in. A steamboat was waiting for them. But they had to wait three days for the snow to end. They sailed across Lake of the Woods. When they got near to North West Angle, they had to break ice for 45 metres just to get to shore.

Once on shore, the men only were 160 kilometres away from Fort Garry. Waiting for them were two types of transportation. One was a covered cart for the officers. The other was a Red River cart. It was loaded with government tents. Unfortunately, the tents could not be used. They were frozen hard.

There was enough food for two meals over the next four days. Their last night was spent at Fort Lachine. They slept on the open prairie in a blizzard. The next morning it was –10 degrees Celsius. They had to start marching for Fort Garry without any food.

The men walked 32 kilometres in bitter cold through deep snow. Their clothing gave them no protection and their boots froze solid. Faces were frozen in places. Some fingers and toes were frostbitten. Some members of the troop wrapped their feet in underwear and shirts just to be able to keep on marching.

Finally, Troop C arrived at Fort Garry. There, they were met by Bishop Tache. He insisted they spend the night in at St. Boniface Cathedral. It was like heaven to the troops. There was hot food and clean sheets on their beds. The next morning it was back out into the cold. They still had the journey to Stone Fort. They would stay there for the winter.

To get there, they had to cross the freshly frozen Red River. It was a dangerous route. But the men had no choice. Finally, the men of Troop C met up with the men of Troop A and Troop B.

It was a cold and cloudy Monday morning on November 3, 1873. That was the day the men of the three troops were sworn in as members of the police force of the North-West. Each gave his promise. He would serve for three years. And he would pay back any damage he might do to property in the line of duty.

The men were given uniforms and guns. They began training immediately.

The First Patrol
The first call for the NWMP came in early December 1873. Word reached Stone Fort that whisky traders were selling liquor to Native peoples. This was happening on the west coast of Lake Winnipeg. Commissioner French assigned Inspector James Macleod to lead a patrol. Macleod selected four NWMP officers and guides to accompany him. After learning how to snowshoe, the patrol set off.

At first, the five men travelled on horse-drawn sleighs. Two dog teams pulled toboggans loaded with a tent, blankets, and food. At the mouth of the Red River, the men snowshoed and mushed for several days. Finally, they reached the log cabin of the whisky traders.

The patrol arrested six men. They took away about 38 litres of liquor. Then they returned to Stone Fort with their prisoners. It was Christmas Eve. The first NWMP patrol had been a success.

The Second Contingent

During the winter of 1873–1874, Commissioner French decided the NWMP needed another 150 men to police the West. John A. Macdonald was no longer prime minister. Alexander Mackenzie was the new prime minister. He agreed to more men. French found 150 more men in Toronto. These men formed Troops D, E, and F.

Recruits had to be 18 years of age. One 15-year-old, Frederick "Fred" Augustus Bagley, applied anyway. He was an experienced horseman. He was accepted as a member of the NWMP and served for the next 25 years.

On June 6, 1874, two special railway cars left Toronto. They headed west. They carried 217 Mounties. Extra men had been hired. That was done in case some didn't like life in the West and decided to leave. They arrived in Fargo, North Dakota, on June 12.

On June 13, the troops rode out on the five-day overland journey to Fort Dufferin (near Pembina, North Dakota). There they would meet the first set of troops. It wasn't an easy journey. The men were woken by a bugle at 4 a.m. Marching started at 5 or 6 a.m. Men and horses were exhausted. Some of the horses died.

Meanwhile, Troops A, B, and C were waiting at Fort Dufferin. When Troops D, E, and F arrived on June 19, there were 300 men together.

Prairie storms can be wicked. The next night a wicked prairie storm blew in. Heavy rain pounded down. Thunder boomed. Lighting sizzled in the sky. The

Constable Fred A. Bagley aged 15

storm scared the horses. They ran. Men tried to stop the horses. Six of the men were trampled. The horses overturned the huge wagons. They dashed through a row of tents. They scattered everything. They all tried to run through the gate at once. They crashed and rolled over one another.

Of the 300 horses, about 250 fled south. They

ran for another 50 to 80 kilometres. A group of riders, including Sam Steele, searched for the runaway horses. Twenty-four hours later, they returned with all but one horse. Fifteen-year-old Fred Bagley had ridden with the searchers. When he returned he was so tired that he fell asleep in his saddle. He had to be lifted off his horse — Old Buck — and put to bed.

Three weeks later, on July 9, 1874, the NWMP was on the move. They headed west to find Fort Whoop-Up, the American trading centre for illegal whisky.

The March West Begins

The story of the march west has been the subject of many books and films. It is an exciting tale.

It was around 5 p.m. on July 9 when the NWMP left Fort Dufferin. The riders stretched out in a line more than four kilometres long. There were 274 Mounties, 20 Métis guides, and 310 horses. Following the riders were 2 mortars, 2 one-ton cannons, 114 oxcarts, 73 wagons, 33 head of beef cattle, 142 work oxen, forges, mowing machines, farming equipment, ploughs, and more.

It was a colourful parade. The Mounties wore their dress uniforms. Dress uniforms were scarlet red jackets, tight-fitting grey pants, pillbox caps or snow-white pith helmets, white gloves, and shining black boots. Each troop rode a different colour horse — dark bays for Troop A, dark browns for B, bright chestnuts for C, greys for D, blacks for E, and light bays for F.

Indeed, the NWMP looked very organized as they marched away from Fort Dufferin. But really, the march was poorly planned. The men were not prepared. The red coats were not practical for prairie conditions. The horses that had been brought from Ontario were not suited for long prairie treks and pulling wagons. They began to die. Many of the guns did not work. And there was no drinking water along the route.

The group travelled an average of 43 kilometres a day at first. Then the weather got hot. Diarrhea became common. With the horses getting weaker, the men had to walk every second hour. This gave the horses a break. But the men's leather boots wore out. Their feet blistered and bled. Some men would piggyback each other.

If they found a spot where there was plenty of water, pasture, and wood, the men could stop for a rest of five days. To lighten the load, sick men and weak horses would join Troop A. Strong horses and men in Troop A would move out. Then Troop A would be sent north to Fort Ellice.

Meanwhile, the main group continued southwest. They followed the route made two years earlier by the men who mapped the border between Canada and the United States. In front were men looking for water and grass for the animals. And stretching back almost 16 kilometres were the slower members on the wagons. There was also the cattle and oxen. Sometimes the slower men got far behind. They would miss dinner. Not that the meals were great. Often a meal was soggy bread, salt bacon, and flapjacks fried in axle grease.

When the horses became too weak to carry any riders, the men walked. Soon the animals were too weak to pull wagons. The Mounties themselves had to haul the wagons up the hills with their own hands. Often there would be no wood or dry buffalo chips for fire fuel. That meant no supper. Everyone went to bed hungry and cold.

Another problem was the guides. An American guide named Morrow had joined them along the march. French suspected that Morrow might be a spy. He thought Morrow might have been sent by the whisky traders. Morrow lead the troops astray.

Things got worse. On September 8, rainstorms and a cold north wind replaced the heat. Five horses died on the night of September 9. French ordered each of the men to give up one of their blankets to cover a horse at night. On September 10, the troops thought they were lost. Everyone was glum.

Finally, the scouts located a fort. But it was not Fort Whoop-Up. They found three broken-down, abandoned cabins. There was no grazing land nearby. French realized how serious this was. Quick action needed to be taken. He had to get the men and horses to safety. In the south, he could see the Sweet Grass Hills near the Montana border. On September 15, the troops headed toward them.

The journey was exhausting. They travelled slowly through cold rain, wind, and sometimes, great buffalo herds. French's decision had been a good one. Three days later they found water and grass. Sadly, a number of the horses died.

While the men headed for the Sweet Grass Hills, French went a different direction. He took Assistant Commissioner Macleod, two officers, guide Pierre Léveillé, plus four carts. They rode 145 kilometres south to Fort Benton, Montana. There they bought supplies and purchased horses. French also used the telegraph services to contact Ottawa. He hired another guide. French also made some decisions.

Troops D and E would head east. They would arrange for winter housing. They would also look into finding permanent headquarters. Macleod would lead Troops B, C, and F to deal with Fort Whoop-Up. There they would stay and build their own fort. If they were there, the whisky traders would not return.

At Fort Benton, there was a telegraph from the Canadian government waiting for French. Ottawa told him to march east to Swan River (near Fort Pelly). There he would find "fine barracks" being built for the NWMP headquarters. French returned to Canada the next day and headed back east.

Macleod stayed at Fort Benton long enough to hire Jerry Potts. Jerry Potts was a short, bowlegged Métis who had great ability to lead as a guide and scout. He also could speak several Native languages. Potts became the force's chief interpreter for the next 22 years.

Potts was no fan of the whisky traders. He had worked at Fort Whoop-Up. He saw the problems that whisky brought to the Native peoples. In fact, his own father, mother, and half-brother had all been murdered because of whisky.

Potts agreed to work for the NWMP for $90 a month. He believed the Mounties were serious about putting an end to whisky smuggling and bringing peace to the West. He liked that. He brought Macleod and the three troops to Fort Whoop-Up. It was an 80-kilometre march. The troops arrived on October 9. They stopped at a river bluff overlooking the "real" Fort Whoop-Up.

Macleod was ready to attack. Potts suggested that they "just ride in." It was strangely quiet. The Mounties approached the fort. Macleod thought it might be a trap. He was prepared for battle.

He positioned the field guns to aim at the fort. He placed the troops in battle lines. Then, when Potts signalled Macleod, the two of them rode up to the huge doors. Macleod knocked. The gate immediately opened. There to greet the two men was the fort's agent, Dave Akers. He invited them to come inside. Then he offered all the Mounties a hot meal and fresh vegetables.

Akers, a Dutch-American, was one of the original whisky traders in the country. He had run away to California when he was young. He had made about

$60,000 in gold dust. The story goes that as he was heading back to the eastern U.S. to marry his girlfriend, his gold dust bag was stolen. Broke, he headed back west.

Macleod ordered his men to search Fort Whoop-Up. They found no liquor on site. It had all been removed. They knew the Mounties were coming. Everyone else left the fort.

Macleod liked the fort. He offered to buy it from Akers for $10,000. He would use it as the new police post. Akers asked for $25,000. Macleod refused.

The NWMP left the next morning. They went to find somewhere to build their own fort. Potts led the men to an island on the Belly River (now the Oldman River). He said it was the best site.

The men then began construction of the new fort. They named it Fort Macleod. It would be the first permanent Mountie post in western Canada.

At the end of 1874, the Mounties had six posts in the West. There was Fort Dufferin, Swan River, Fort Garry, Fort Ellice, Fort Edmonton, and Fort Macleod.

Chapter 2
Prairie Policing

By 1875, the Mounties had stopped most of the illegal whisky trade in western Canada. Next they had to focus on bringing law and order to the northwest. They needed to help new settlers in the area. And they needed to help develop positive relationships with the Native peoples of the Prairies.

Making peace with Native leaders was important. It helped make the Prairies a safer place to live. The government had another reason to make peace. They wanted the area's Native leaders to sign treaties. These treaties would state that the Native peoples would give their land to the federal government.

Crowfoot and Red Crow
The mounted policemen were ordered by the Canadian

government to establish friendly relations with the Native peoples of the West.

James Macleod was given the task of befriending the Native chiefs. James Macleod was born on the Isle of Skye in Scotland. Macleod had immigrated to Upper Canada with his parents when he was nine years old. He became a lawyer at the age of 26. In 1873, he joined the NWMP as one of the original nine officers. When he had joined he already had 18 years of militia experience. Macleod participated in the 1870 Red River Rebellion.

He had marched west and survived the search for Fort Whoop-Up. The skills he needed now were not physical and survival skills. They were people skills. Macleod had to gain the support of the Blackfoot Confederacy. This alliance was made up of the Blackfoot (Siksika), Blood (Kainaiwa), Peigan (Piikani), Sarcee (Tsuu T'ina), and Stoney (Bearspaw, Chiniki, Wesley, Goodstoney) tribes.

It would be up to him to convince the chiefs that the NWMP had come in peace as their friends. They had not come as enemies.

If Native leaders like the powerful Chief Crowfoot of the Blackfoot or Chief Red Crow of the Blood chose to, they could fight the NWMP. The Prairies could become a war land. This is what happened in the United States.

Would the chiefs agree to listen or would they choose to go to war? Macleod knew his relationship with them would play a huge role in their decision.

The Mounties began to build their fort.

The first chiefs who came to visit Macleod at the fort were from the Blood and Peigan tribes. Perhaps they were sent by Crowfoot to spy and bring back information. Macleod met with them. Jerry Potts helped explain that the Mounties had come to get rid of the whisky traders and bring peace to their country.

Then the powerful Red Crow visited Macleod. He wanted to know how the NWMP would work. Macleod explained it to him. The Mounties believed in justice for all, regardless of race. Red Crow promised to cooperate.

Macleod was hoping that Crowfoot, the leader of the Blackfoot, would soon visit. Crowfoot was known for his wisdom and bravery. His word was law in the southern Prairies.

Finally, on December 1, 1874, Crowfoot rode into Fort Macleod. He came to visit Stamix Otokan or "Bull's Head." It was the name given to Macleod by the Blackfoot. Macleod knew that the great chief was coming to visit. He welcomed him with honour. All of his men were wearing their scarlet dress uniforms.

Crowfoot made it clear that he was there as neither friend nor foe. Rather, he had come with an open mind. He was willing to hear about these men riding horses and wearing scarlet uniforms. Why had they come? What were they going to do? How long were they planning to stay? A powwow would be held a few days later. Macleod was expected to give his answers.

When Crowfoot returned, he brought with him the mightiest of the Peigan and Blood chiefs. After introductions, they shook hands. They sat in a circle. Jerry Potts lit the peace pipe and passed it around. Serious dialogue began.

The chiefs had come to hear Macleod talk. With Potts acting as his interpreter, Macleod said, "I come from the Great White Queen [Queen Victoria]. I come in friendship."

Macleod explained. The Mounties had come to the Prairies to stop whisky trading. They were there to bring peace and order. They brought with them laws from the Great White Queen. He told the chiefs that the NWMP would stay at Fort Macleod. They would enforce the Queen's laws. They would punish anyone — white or Native — who broke the laws.

Macleod promised the chiefs that no Native people would be punished if they did not understand the law. They would not be punished for actions that they did not know to be wrong. He then told them that murder, horse stealing, and war were wrong. These crimes had to stop.

Finally, Macleod made something clear to the chiefs. The Mounties had not come to steal the Native peoples' land. If the government wanted any land, it would send men to discuss and make treaties with the Native peoples.

The 44-year-old Crowfoot listened. Then, after a long silence, Crowfoot spoke. "My brother, your words make me glad. I listened to them not only with my ears but with my heart also. In the coming of the Long Knives, with their firewater and quick-shooting guns, we are weak and our people have been woefully slain and impoverished. You say this will be stopped. We are glad to have it stopped. What you tell us about this strong power which will govern good law and treat the Indian same as the white man, makes us glad to hear. My brother, I believe you and I am thankful."

Treaty Negotiations

Chief Crowfoot's influence and power was evident. Three years later talks began for Treaty Seven. Talks were between the chiefs of the Blackfoot Confederacy and the Canadian government. Lieutenant Governor David Laird and NWMP Commissioner James Macleod acted for the government.

On September 19, 1877, at Blackfoot Crossing on the Bow River, Crowfoot and the chiefs met with Laird and Macleod. There were 4000 to 5000 Native peoples gathered. They waited. For the next few days, Macleod and Laird answered questions. Questions about the ownership of the Native reserves were asked. What were the timber and coal rights? What were the Native rights to hunt over the Prairies?

The government would offer reserves to the Native peoples and assistance. All they had to do in return was give their land to the government.

On September 21, in the early afternoon, a hush fell over the crowd. Crowfoot rose to make his announcement. Would he sign the treaty or not? He spoke. "If the police had not come to this country, where would we all be now? Bad men and whisky were killing us so fast that very few of us would have been alive today. The Mounted Police have protected us as the feathers of the bird protect it from the frosts of winter. I wish all my people good and trust that all our hearts will increase in goodness from this time forward. I am satisfied. I am satisfied. I will sign the Treaty."

Next, Red Crow spoke. He felt the offer was not ideal. He was not sure he wanted to sign. He and Crowfoot had spent the night talking about the treaty. But now he had made up his mind. "Three years ago when the Mounted Police came to my country, I met and shook hands with Stamix Otokan at the Belly River. Since then he has made me many promises and kept them all — not one of them has been broken. Everything that the Mounted Police have done has been for our good. I trust Stamix Otokan and will leave everything to him."

The other chiefs also agreed. The next day, September 22, Treaty Seven was officially signed.

Until his death on April 25, 1890, Crowfoot kept his word to stand by the NWMP. When American Sioux asked Crowfoot to join in violence against Canadian white people, he refused. When Louis Riel tried to find support from Crowfoot for the 1885 North-West

Rebellion, Crowfoot refused once again.

Red Crow also continued to follow the path of peace. "We have had enough war. I think we can live without it. If civilization can tame the buffalo so that they are like cattle, the lesson is one that I should not forget."

Crowfoot and Red Crow were both intelligent leaders. They had vision. If the NWMP had not been able to gain their friendship and support, it would have been difficult — perhaps impossible — for the Mounties to bring change to western Canada without violence.

The American Sioux Arrive

The feeling of peace was soon threatened. The American Sioux were enemies of many Canadian Native peoples. They had come to Canada.

In the United States, there was much violence between the Native peoples, white settlers, and the government. For years, the American Sioux had been fighting to stop white settlers from taking their land. In 1875, they were ordered to leave. They had to leave or be called enemies of the United States. The Sioux refused to leave. So the United States Army stepped in.

In June 1876, the situation became deadly. There was battle called the Battle of Little Big Horn. It was fought between the Sioux and five companies of the 7th U.S. Cavalry. Lieutenant Colonel George A. Custer was in command. On June 25, the Sioux trapped and killed all 265 soldiers and civilians in Custer's group. This massacre was led by Chief Sitting Bull.

What happened next was very important in Canadian history. The key players were Inspector James Walsh and Chief Sitting Bull. Walsh was in command of both Fort Walsh and the nearby Wood Mountain unit. Chief Sitting Bull was the most feared and powerful chief in North America.

The NWMP were ready for the American Sioux if they fled to Canada. In late November 1876, news reached Fort Walsh that a large party of Sioux was moving north toward Wood Mountain. Walsh and 15 Mounties rode eight days from Fort Walsh to get to the site. By the time they got there, it was early December. About 3000 Sioux, along with 3500 horses and 30 U.S. government mules, were camped close to the nearby trading post.

Walsh and his men rode right into the camp. They asked to speak to Chief Black Moon. The Sioux called a council and explained. They were tired of being hunted. They had come to the land of the Great White Mother to find refuge. Walsh listened. Then he laid out some rules. If they wanted to stay in Canada, they would have to follow some rules. The rules were to obey Canadian laws. They had to keep peace with Canadian Native peoples. Finally, they could not use Canada as a base to attack the United States.

For the rest of the winter, the NWMP patrolled the area as they waited for Sitting Bull to arrive.

Walsh and Sitting Bull

In May 1877, the NWMP received word that Sitting Bull had settled 95 kilometres southeast of Fort Walsh. Inspector Walsh immediately rode out to meet him. He took with him Sergeant Robert McCutcheon, three constables, and two scouts.

On May 7, three days after leaving the fort, Walsh and his men were following Sitting Bull's trail until they came upon the edge of a Native camp. Calmly, they stopped and sat on their horses while a group of Sioux riders approached them.

Spotted Eagle, one of the chiefs, told them they were the first white men to ride into Sitting Bull's camp. Walsh asked to meet Sitting Bull. A short while later the famous chief arrived.

He looked to be in his forties. He was muscular. He stood at 5 feet, 10 inches. He was bowlegged and walked with a limp. His eyes were alert. His features were sharp. Two braids of black hair hung down his shoulders. He greeted his visitors with handshakes.

The Mounties and the Sioux talked the rest of the day. When Sitting Bull was asked why he had come to Canada, he said to find peace in the White Mother's land.

Walsh explained Canadian laws to Sitting Bull. He insisted that Canadian laws had to be obeyed by everyone. Sitting Bull liked what Walsh told him about the White Mother's laws, especially that everyone would be treated equally.

Walsh and his men stayed the night in Sitting Bull's camp. All seemed to go well, until the next morning. Five horses were being brought into the Sioux camp. They were being led by White Dog. He was known to be a great warrior.

Solomon and the other police scout, Léveillé, knew the three horses. They belonged to Father DeCorty of Cypress Hills. McCutcheon walked over to White Dog to arrest him. He was standing with a group of 50 to 60 warriors. White Dog refused to be arrested. Hundreds of Sioux were curious to see what would happen next.

White Dog was sure that the Mounties wouldn't dare take him away. But he was wrong.

"Tell me where you got those horses, how you got them, and what you intend doing with them, or I'll clap these irons on you and take you away," said Walsh. He dangled leg irons in front of White Dog.

A hush fell over the camp. White Dog had expected the Sioux to rescue him. His courage weakened when they didn't.

He said that the horses were lost. He explained that in America the finder got to keep a lost horse until someone claimed it.

Although Walsh did not believe him, he released White Dog. White Dog turned to walk away. He muttered in his own language, "I shall meet you again."

Angry, Walsh stopped. He ordered White Dog to repeat his words to the interpreter. White Dog refused.

He stood silently. Walsh asked him again, and again White Dog kept quiet. Then, lifting the leg irons high, Walsh said, "White Dog, withdraw those words, or I shall put you in irons and take you to Fort Walsh for threatening a police officer."

White Dog apologized. He said his words were not meant to be a threat. Walsh knew he was lying. He accepted the apology. He felt he had made an example. The Sioux people had seen he had not backed down. He had not shown fear. His message was clear. They must obey Canadian law.

Sitting Bull did not leave Canada and surrender to American military authorities until July 18, 1881. Three years later, he was killed by tribal police.

Despite their differences, Walsh and Sitting Bull had a strong friendship. Walsh felt that Americans did not understand Sitting Bull. He was not a cruel man. He was kind. He was not dishonest. He was truthful. He loved his people. He was a good friend.

Handling Trouble
Within days of returning to Fort Walsh, Inspector Walsh again rode out to meet American Native peoples. But this time, it was to stop violence being committed against Canadian Native peoples.

The problem began when a group of American Assiniboine had crossed into Canada to hunt buffalo. This group had set their 250 lodges beside the 15 lodges of a Saulteaux camp. An Assiniboine warrior named Crow's Dance was threatening. He demanded obedience from Saulteaux Chief Little Child. The Saulteaux leader refused. He explained that he obeyed the laws of the "White Chief of Fort Walsh." He then ordered his people to start breaking up their camp. They were going to move away.

Angry, the Assiniboine attacked the Saulteaux. They fired guns and killed 19 sled dogs. They slashed teepees and knocked down anyone who got in the way. Crow's Dance then warned the Saulteaux, "And if the redcoats come, we'll cut out the White Chief's heart and eat it."

The tough talk didn't scare Little Child. He rode 80 kilometres to report the event to the NWMP. Walsh rode back with Little Child. Fifteen Mounties came with him. So did scout Louis Léveillé. They stopped when they could see the Assiniboine camp about two kilometres away. It was in a valley below.

Walsh ordered the pistols to be loaded. He surrounded the camp with some of the ready men. Then, silently in the night, Walsh and the rest of the men rode down toward the camp. They quickly seized Crow's Dance and another chief by the name of Crooked Arm. They also took some other men. They carried them to where the other Mounties were waiting.

The prisoners were handcuffed. It was only 5 a.m. The rest of the Assiniboine in the camp slept.

The next morning, Walsh sent Léveillé back to the

camp to ask the other Assiniboine chiefs to come to a meeting. When they did, they brought along an angry crowd of Assiniboine. Walsh told them that the law allowed people to move when they wanted to move. He demanded that the Assiniboine would never again force their will on the Saulteaux.

The NWMP took Crow's Dance and 12 others as prisoners. Later, Walsh released 11 of the warriors with a warning. Crow's Dance and Chief Crooked Arm received short prison terms.

The Deadly Power of the Windigo

In March 1879, a tall, muscular Cree by the name of Swift Runner arrived at the Roman Catholic mission at St. Albert. He reported that nine members of his family had died that winter. His wife and children had all died of starvation.

The priests knew that the past winter had been very cold. With no buffalo herds to hunt, many Native people were starving. But they did not quite believe Swift Runner's story. He looked healthy. He said he had survived by chewing rawhide. He had made tea by boiling his teepee.

The priests allowed Swift Runner to stay. Reverend Father Hippolyte Leduc listened to his tale. The Cree man told of nightmares. An evil spirit of the Windigo was trying to possess him. The priests became alarmed. They asked the NWMP at Fort Saskatchewan to find out how Swift Runner's family had actually died.

In Native mythology, the Windigo is an evil spirit. It possesses a person and causes him or her to want to eat human flesh. Once the evil spirit tasted human flesh, it only craved more. Many believe, that once possessed, that person had to be burned to ashes. Only this would stop the evil spirit's hunger.

The priests did not believe Swift Runner's story about his family dying of starvation. Neither did Inspector William D. Jarvis. On May 27, Jarvis arrested the Cree man for murder. He brought him to Fort Saskatchewan. There he asked questions. Swift Runner stuck to his story. The NWMP organized a search party to gather evidence. They went to his winter camp near the Sturgeon River.

Swift Runner was shackled inside a Red River cart. Twice he tried to escape. Twice he was captured. He insisted that his family had died of starvation. When they arrived in the area of the camp, Swift Runner led the Mounties in circles.

Finally, the Métis interpreter made a drink. It was a drink made of plug tobacco soaked in strong tea. He explained that the "medicine" would make Swift Runner tell them everything. The interpreter was right.

After taking the drink, Swift Runner "threw back his head, howled like a wolf and led the police to a camp in the bush." It was a horrible death camp. Human skulls and bones were scattered around the campfire ashes. A nearby cooking pot was coated with human fat. Horrified, the Mounties realized that Swift Runner had killed and eaten his entire family.

Swift Runner was charged with murder. He was sentenced to die on December 20.

Before Swift Runner went to trial, he confessed to the murders. He felt it was not his fault. He was possessed by the spirit of the Windigo.

While he was in custody, Swift Runner behaved strangely. At times he joked about his crime. He told the guard "what fine eating he would make." It was –42 degrees Celsius when Swift Runner was hanged on the morning of December 20.

Swift Runner was the first person to be executed by the NWMP.

The First Murder

The first murder of a Mountie happened in 1879. Young Constable Marmaduke Graburn was 18 years old when he joined the NWMP in Ottawa. Graburn was posted for duty at the fort's main horse camp.

On the afternoon of November 17, 1879, Graburn had an argument with a Blood man called Star Child. Star Child was begging for food at the horse camp. Graburn told the man to leave. Later, Graburn was missing. His horse was saddled but there was no rider.

A search party was led by Jerry Potts. The party

followed a bloody trail. The trail led them to Graburn's body. He had been shot twice through the back of the head. The murder was hard to investigate. A chinook wind had swept through the area. Snow had melted. No tracks could be followed.

Six months later, two Bloods were arrested for stealing horses. They were worried that they might be blamed for Graburn's murder. They decided to tell the police the name of the murderer. It was midnight.

The two prisoners said it was Star Child who murdered the Mountie. He had fled across the border for safety. He now lived in the Bear Paw Mountains. The Mounties asked the United States sheriff to arrest Star Child. The sheriff wanted $5000 first. The NWMP refused to pay him. Star Child remained safe in the United States.

A year later, Star Child returned to Canada. He joined the Blood Nation near Fort Macleod. Five Mounties, including Corporal Patterson and Potts, launched a surprise attack to arrest him. It was at dawn. They entered his lodge. He saw them and shot his rifle. Quickly, Patterson picked Star Child up and carried him out to his horse.

The NWMP rode out of the camp. Blood warriors were right behind them. At full gallop for 40 kilometres, the police raced to Fort Macleod. They tried hard to keep ahead. It was hard. The ride was exhausting. They knew their lives were at risk. Thankfully, they won the race to the fort's gate.

At his trial, Star Child confessed to the murder. But the jury found him not guilty. They were afraid of the Blood. The first murder of a Mountie to die a violent death while on duty was recorded as, "Murdered by person or persons unknown ..."

Not long after his first trial, Star Child was convicted of horse stealing. He was sentenced to 14 years in Stony Mountain Penitentiary. After, the NWMP hired him as a scout.

Constable Graburn is buried at Fort Walsh. In Cypress Hills Park, it is marked where he died. At the Beechwood Cemetery in Ottawa, his stone reads "Marmaduke Graburn — *Primus Moriri* [First to die]."

Chapter 3
Policing the Klondike

Before the 1890s, justice in the Yukon was decided at local miners' meetings. Everyone had one vote. Decisions were made by voting.

The first Yukon miners' meeting was held around 1886. Whisky traders began to appear in the area in the 1890s. After that, the miners moved their meetings to saloons. There they could drink while voting.

The federal government sent Inspector Charles Constantine to the Yukon in 1894 to report on the conditions there. Constantine had been part of the 1870 Red River Expedition alongside Sam Steele, James Macleod, and James Walsh. He was appointed Manitoba's chief of police that same year. Constantine joined the NWMP in 1885. Before he had served in a volunteer military regiment during the 1885 Riel Rebellion.

Constantine gave his report. The Yukon could be controlled if at least 50 men were sent. The government agreed to send 19 men. The following summer, Constantine returned to the Yukon.

In July of 1895, Inspector Constantine, his wife, and a NWMP group left for the North. They travelled by boat up the Pacific Coast and then up the Yukon River. Once they arrived near Dawson City, they started to build their new headquarters.

By November, nine buildings were finished. None of them were very comfortable. Inside, winter temperatures averaged zero. The mud roofs leaked dirty water. The new police post was called Fort Constantine.

Inspector Constantine and his men quickly got to work. They had many jobs to do. They investigated crimes. They collected customs duties, gold royalties, and miners' fees. The men also spent time looking for smuggled liquor. They acted as coroners. And they delivered the mail.

A year after the Mounties' arrival, the Klondike Gold Rush began. A miner named George Carmack and his party, Tagish Charley and Skookum Jim, discovered gold on Rabbit Creek. The NWMP prepared themselves for the gold seekers.

During the winters of 1897 and 1898, tens of thousands of prospectors arrived from around the world to seek their fortune. Inspector Constantine requested more Mounties. He got them. By 1898, there were

10 officers and 254 men serving in the Yukon. Now the NWMP had a chain of posts from Checkout all the way to Dawson City.

Building a Road to Nowhere

In 1897, Inspector Constantine wanted to build a road from Edmonton to the Yukon. This would be an easier route for Canadians to use to travel to the Klondike.

The Canadian government looked into building the road. Fifty-five-year-old Inspector J. D. Moodie was to lead. Moodie chose his patrol carefully. These men would need survival skills and energy to complete the long trek into unknown wilderness. He selected Constable Frank J. Fitzgerald and Special Constables Richard Hardisty, Frank Lafferty, and H. S. Tobin. He also hired Baptiste Pepin to manage the pack train of 31 horses.

This group of men had many tasks. They had to make a map showing the best route from Edmonton to the Pelly River. The map had to include the best trail for wagons, good grazing sites, and hunting areas. It also had to identify hills, ditches, and where bridges needed to be built. In addition, the men had to collect information for an "everything-you-need-to-know" information package for future travellers of the route.

Commissioner Herschmer laid out the wilderness-breaking route they would follow: Edmonton to Peace River to Fort St. John. Across the Rockies to Finlay River. North along Finlay River to Fort Grahame. Then over

Sifton Pass to Sylvester Landing on the Dease River. Once they reached the Dease River, it would be up to Moodie to choose the final route to the Pelly River. There was no room for failure. They just had to do it.

Moodie and his men left Edmonton on September 8, 1897. It would take them 14 months. They would travel in all kinds of weather.

The men chopped their way through fallen trees. They slashed through brush. They found lost horses. They made bridges and crossed raging rivers. They trekked through thick muskeg.

When the small group of Mounties reached the fast-moving Peace River, they built a raft to cross it. The current swept the raft 450 metres downstream. This forced the men to pull it back upstream by hand. Next they had to swim the horses across the cold swift waters. But only 10 of the 31 horses would cross. The others refused to enter the river. The men had to leave them on the other side. They got help at nearby Fort St. John. Later, the Mounties returned to the horses with an HBC flat-bottomed riverboat. Using ropes, they led them across the river.

After buying an additional 33 dogs and 5 sleighs, the patrol left Fort St. John on December 2. By the end of December, they had to kill some of their horses in order to feed the dogs.

It was a brutal journey. The snow was deep. They had to walk around canyons. They were exhausted. The men got lost at one point and travelled 45 kilometres off course. It was very cold. The temperature hovered between –34 and –40 degrees Celsius. Sickness and accidents were common. On four occasions, Moodie suffered from snow blindness.

They ran out of food. Luckily, they soon reached Fort Grahame. At the fort there was food for the men, but none for the dogs. The Mounties had to go ice fishing for the dog food.

Still, there was not enough food. Moodie decided to go south and get more supplies. He took four men with him. During the trip, Moodie got terrible snow blindness. His eyes were bandaged for four days. He had to be pulled on a sleigh.

On July 7, 1898, more than two months later, the five men returned. They had food. Eight days later, the patrol continued toward the Pelly River. They had to borrow packhorses as they had killed all their own horses to feed the dogs. It would take them four months to finally reach the Pelly River.

By this time, they had been on the patrol for 13 months. Many had thought the group had died. They hadn't, but they still had a ways to go. Now they would have to travel downstream to Fort Selkirk.

The weary party started paddling their canvas canoe down the Pelly River. The rapids and floating ice put holes in the canoe. Two men and some supplies moved to a small raft. The raft sunk. They built a bigger raft. But it was too big to get through frozen waterways.

Finally, luck came their way. A group of men were on their way north to the Klondike. Moodie was able to purchase their Peterborough canoe for $450.

The river started to freeze and the men were almost sucked underneath the strong current. Moodie ordered the men off the water. They were exhausted, hungry, and cold. They still had 65 kilometres to travel to get to Fort Selkirk.

Desperate, they left almost everything behind. They walked the rest of the way.

Two days and nights later, the exhausted patrol reached Fort Selkirk on October 24. They had travelled 14 months and 2500 kilometres since leaving Edmonton.

The route was too treacherous. The Canadian government stopped working on it — for a while.

Ton of Goods

In 1897, as Moodie and his men were beginning to build the road, ex-Inspector James M. Walsh arrived in the Klondike. He came to serve as the territory's first commissioner. By that time, Walsh had been away from policing for 15 years and had been working as a coal dealer in Winnipeg. Now he was responsible for the NWMP in the Yukon.

He arrived in early winter. River ice forced his government party to stay the winter near Big Salmon. They

Canadian customs house at the summit of Chilkoot Pass,
Alaska. Note the piles of supplies — the NWMP would not
allow prospectors into the Yukon without enough food
and supplies to last the winter.

had few supplies. He made it a rule that anyone travelling to the Yukon had to be prepared. If they did not
have a year's supply of food and equipment, they were
turned back. This rule became known as the famous
"ton of goods" criteria. Each person had to have 1.4 kilos
of food per day, plus equipment and tools.

Early in 1898, the NWMP set up units at Chilkoot
Pass and White Pass. They were right on the border

between Canada and the United States. The police were there to collect customs duty. They made sure each person had a "ton of goods." They wanted everyone to know that they had to obey Canadian laws.

Sam Steele, Lion of the North

In February 1898, the "Lion of the North," Sam Steele, arrived in the Yukon. Steele was already a legend.

Born in Upper Canada in 1849, he was known as one of the "original" Mounties. He had joined the NWMP at its start in 1873. Now he was 49 years old. He had served the NWMP for 25 years. He had done the march west in 1874. He had been part of the North-West Rebellion of 1885. And he had helped build the Canadian Pacific Railway through the Rockies.

He was tall, barrel-chested, handsome, and coura-geous. He was the heroic image of the Mountie. A man of action, he was a strong leader. He was both respected and feared.

Steele had been serving in southern Alberta when he received his orders to go north. It was in January 1898, and the Yukon was gold-rush crazy.

In late March of 1898, Steele climbed the summit of White Pass. He went down the Canadian side to Lake Bennett. He found more than 10,000 people camped on both sides of the lake. They were building boats and waiting for the Yukon River to thaw.

A huge crowd on the Yukon River would be

dangerous. The NWMP needed to know the details of each boat. He ordered that every boat have a number painted clearly on it. The NWMP recorded each number in a register. They also recorded the names of every man, woman, and child onboard. They made a note of the names and addresses of next of kin.

When the lake became clear of ice on May 29, Steele counted more than 800 boats on Lake Bennett. Steele knew the most dangerous part of the river journey was yet to come. The next day, he boarded the small steamer *Kilbourne* and took the river route to Miles Canyon. It was a deep and dangerous gorge. There were steep cliffs of granite on either side. The river ran swiftly.

When Steele arrived at Miles Canyon, he was greeted by several thousand boats.

Some boats had foolishly rushed ahead. The rapids were too dangerous. Up to 150 boats had been smashed to pieces on the rocks. Ten men had drowned. Corporal Dixon and the Mounties had risked their lives to rescue men, women, and children from the cold, fast-moving waters. Sadly, they could not save everyone.

To prevent more tragedy, Steele quickly made a plan. No woman or child would be allowed in any boat or canoe. Instead, they would have to walk the eight kilometres to the foot of the rapids. Every boat would be inspected and had to have a river pilot to guide the boat through the canyon. The NWMP hired the guides.

The crowd liked what they heard. They got back

into their boats and obeyed Steele's orders. No more lives were lost in Miles Canyon.

Bringing Out the Gold

One of the jobs the NWMP had during the Klondike Gold Rush was to collect custom duties on the gold found. They collected more than $150,000 in gold and notes. This money was good for the government. But it posed a problem for the NWMP.

How could they safely transfer so much money and gold to Victoria, BC? The Alaskan towns of Dyea and Skagway were full of crime. How could they safely get so much money and gold past the gangster Soapy Smith and his men?

Sam Steele chose Inspector Zachary Taylor Wood to carry out the secret delivery. His mission would take him on a route over the Chilkoot summit to Dyea. From there a boat would take him to Skagway. Then a steamer would be waiting to take him to Victoria.

The NWMP would escort Wood and his small group of men to the Chilkoot summit. After that, the group was on its own. Wood packed the gold and money in ordinary Mountie kit bags. They decided to spread a rumour about why they were leaving. The rumour was that Wood was being sent back to the Prairies. He was leaving the Klondike with his baggage and "boatmen."

Jefferson "Soapy" Smith was a famous criminal. He ruled the Yukon town Skagway. He had his own army, a spy service, and secret police. Soapy ran crooked gambling halls and fake businesses. He had a freight company that didn't haul anything. He never missed an opportunity to rob someone. Inspector Wood knew that Soapy would be willing to kill just about anyone to get his hands on the $150,000 in gold and notes.

Wood and his men left Dawson City on June 9, 1898. Everything was fine until they reached the town of Dyea. There they hired a small boat to cross the bay to the town of Skagway. A boatload of Soapy's thugs tried to run the men down. They didn't back off until Wood threatened to shoot them.

There was more trouble waiting for Wood on the Skagway wharf. Soapy and more of his gunmen were on the dock. Luckily, there were also sailors waiting for him. And they had guns. Soapy hadn't seen the sailors yet. He and his gang were pushing their way through the wharf's crowd toward Wood.

Soapy and Wood came face to face. Both men had their guns ready. Wood remained calm. Then Soapy saw the sailors surrounding him. He backed off.

It would be the last time Wood saw Soapy. A month later, Soapy and another man were both killed in a gunfight.

Chapter 4
Pushing Into
the Arctic

With the Klondike Gold Rush over, life settled down in the Yukon. Regular duties took over. Crime was investigated. Drunks were managed. Prisoners were guarded and trappers were checked on. Mounties also helped other government agencies collect fees. They gave out licences and collected customs and taxes. They took censuses and handle mail at isolated posts.

In 1903, the NWMP began to move deeper into the Canadian North. Two patrols brought law and order beyond the Arctic Circle. One patrol would sail to Hudson Bay. They would set up in the eastern Arctic. Led by Inspector J. D. Moodie, this 16-man patrol left Halifax on the SS *Neptune* on August 22. By the fall, they had successfully built a post at Fullerton.

The other patrol was headed up by Superintendent Charles Constantine. They would go deep into the western Arctic and subarctic through the Mackenzie River system.

The Western Arctic Patrol

In May 1903, Superintendent Constantine left Fort Saskatchewan. With him left 34-year-old Sergeant Frank Fitzgerald, four constables (S. S. Munroe, F. D. Sutherland, R. H. Walker, and John Galpin), and Special Constable Joseph Belrose. They would be building a new police post at Fort McPherson. They might build another on Herschel Island.

There had been complaints that American whaling ships were using Herschel Island as a winter stopover. They had brought alcohol to the Inuit population. Constantine assigned Fitzgerald the command of both the Fort McPherson and Herschel Island posts.

Fort McPherson was a desolate place in 1903. Located on the Peel River, it stood almost 160 kilometres from the Arctic Ocean. The Hudson's Bay Company had five buildings at Fort McPherson. All but one were run-down. There was also a church, a missionary house, and a few Inuit huts there. Dogs overran much of the village. Even in July, the place was cold and uninviting.

Constantine rented several vacant buildings for $45 for three months. He then returned to Fort Saskatchewan. Before leaving, he gave Sergeant Fitzgerald two orders.

The first order was to go to Herschel Island as soon as possible. He was to see if the American whalers or Inuit were still there. Then, he was to establish a police post on the island. The second order was to develop the best all-Canadian route from Fort McPherson to Dawson City. This would allow Fitzgerald and his men to have communications with the outside world. He did not want his men to feel alone.

Fitzgerald had joined the NWMP at the age of 18. Nine years later he had been part of the famous 14-month patrol that had tried to build a route from Edmonton to the Klondike.

Two weeks later, Fitzgerald, Sutherland, and their interpreter, Thompson, sailed to Herschel Island. It took them 10 days to make the 420-kilometre trip. At one point, they had to battle 130-kilometre-per-hour winds on the Arctic Ocean.

Herschel Island is a barren piece of rock. It is about 20 kilometres long and 5 kilometres wide. Sir John Franklin had sighted the island on July 17, 1826. He named the island after Sir John Hersch, a well-known British chemist and astronomer. Hersch and Franklin were friends.

The island had no trees or brush. It did have six warehouse buildings. Four buildings were owned by the Pacific Steam Whaling Company. One was owned by an Anglican mission. There were also 15 sod houses.

When whaling was at its peak in 1893–1894, about

1500 people lived on Herschel Island. Now, almost 10 years later, about 67 men remained. Six more ships were about to arrive. Onboard were more than 250 men looking to spend the winter on the island.

Whaling was big business. Whalebone was worth $10,000 in the 1890s. In a 17-year span from 1889 to 1906, whalers took around 1345 whales out of Canadian waters.

As the whaling captains came ashore on Herschel Island, the two Mounties in their scarlet tunics greeted each one. Politely but bluntly, Fitzgerald let the whalers know that Canadian law must be obeyed. He warned them that they could no longer supply liquor to the Inuit. He also explained that Canadian customs duties would be collected. The crusty captains agreed.

A few weeks later, Fitzgerald and Sutherland made the dangerous return to Fort McPherson. A two-day storm broke their boat into pieces. They were forced to camp on a sandspit. A passing Inuit whaleboat took them the rest of the way. Saltwater had ruined most of their supplies. They were left only with a little flour, a few rabbits, and falling snow for water.

Soon after arriving at Fort McPherson, Fitzgerald prepared to return to Herschel Island. He felt he had to be there to keep an eye on the whalers.

On Herschel Island, Fitzgerald bought two sod houses and a storehouse for winter living. He purchased five tons of coal from one of the whaling boats.

Fitzgerald was based on the island for several years.

Fitzgerald handled an interesting situation while living on the island. It involved famous explorer–anthropologist Vilhjalmur Stefansson in 1908. Stefansson had been sent by the Canadian government and the American Museum of Natural History. He was to study the Inuit. He travelled light. He had forgotten to include matches in his supplies.

The party needed matches to make it through the winter. Captain James Wing of the *Karluk* supplied Stefansson with 1000 matches. But there were smokers in his group. They refused to continue their Arctic journey until they had more matches. Stefansson decided to wait and buy matches from the supply ships expected to arrive shortly at Herschel Island. They never arrived.

Desperate, Stefansson pleaded with Fitzgerald to give him more matches. Fitzgerald refused. He wanted Stefansson to forget about his winter expedition. He did not feel Stefansson was prepared. His party carried no food supplies. They were expected to live off the land. This would likely cause them to starve. Then they would need to be rescued.

Fitzgerald promised the men a cabin and supplies if they remained on Herschel Island for the winter. He said that if they chose to leave, he would not provide them with matches. Stefansson refused the offer.

A few days later, he and his group left. They sailed west to Point Barrow where the men bought matches.

They also bought enough food to last the whole winter.

Fitzgerald was one of the true "Northern Men" of the Mounties. But the dark winter and cold isolation of the Arctic did affect him. In 1909 he wrote, "When there are no ships wintering at Herschel Island, I think that it is one of the most lonesome places on earth. There is no place one can go, except to visit a few hungry natives, and there is no white man to visit nearer than 180 miles [290 km]."

Despite this isolation, Fitzgerald fell in love with an Inuit woman named Lena Oonalina. He was not allowed to marry her. In the summer of 1909, he and Lena had a child. They named her Annie. She was baptized by the island's Anglican minister, Reverend W. H. Fry. Annie was born with a disability. She died at Hay River when she was just 18.

At Fort McPherson and Herschel Island, Fitzgerald had established the world's most northerly police post. Soon, he would face many more obstacles.

The Lost Patrol

On December 21, 1910, Inspector Fitzgerald headed out on his patrol between Fort McPherson and Dawson City. It was a distance of 800 kilometres. It was just another routine winter patrol.

Leaving Fort McPherson with Fitzgerald were Constable George Frances Kinney (27), Constable Richard O'Hara Taylor (28), and Special Constable Sam

Carter (41), an ex-Mountie of 21 years. The men carried with them more than 270 kilos of supplies per sled. Supplies included bacon, salt, milk in tins, flour, dried fruit, beans, coffee and tea, baking powder, and sugar.

When the patrol set out on December 21, the weather conditions were terrible. There was ice fog and heavy snows. On Christmas Day, there was heavy mist and a northwest wind. The temperature hovered around –35 degrees Celsius. The patrol camped with several Native families. Fitzgerald hired a Native man, Esau. He broke trail and guided them. On New Year's Day, Fitzgerald paid Esau $24 for his services. His job was done.

The cold continued. So did the heavy snowstorms. On January 8, the temperature dipped to –55 degrees Celsius with strong headwinds. It was so cold that the men's breath froze on their faces. Four days later, Fitzgerald and his group were lost. Days passed, and still the party was lost. The men became desperate.

They had only 4½ kilos of flour and 3½ kilos of bacon and some dried fish. Their last hope was gone.

The men started to head back to Fort McPherson. That night, they were forced to kill their first dog. It fed the other dogs. The men ate small pieces of bannock and dried fish. On January 19, they killed their second dog.

The temperature warmed up to –29 degrees Celsius, but it was still windy and snowy. The men were almost out of their supplies. They were forced to eat dog meat.

By January 22, the temperature had fallen to –53 degrees Celsius. It was misty and windy.

By February 1, 8 of the 15 sled dogs had been killed for food. On February 5, Fitzgerald wrote in his diary. It would be his last journal entry. It was too cold and windy. His foot was frozen. There were only five dogs left. Everyone's skin was peeling.

At first no one had worried about Fitzgerald and his men. Fitzgerald was an expert. He had travelled and survived many times. But then, Superintendent Snyder started to make plans to look for the missing men.

On February 28, 1911, a search party was sent out from Dawson City. It included Corporal William John "Jack" Dempster.

Despite bad weather, the search party covered the patrol's route in record time. Dempster found some of Fitzgerald's night camps. On March 19, while at Colin Vitisk's cabin on the Peel River, Dempster found some packages. The packages consisted of Fitzgerald's dispatch and mailbags.

Two days later, Dempster found an abandoned toboggan and two sets of dog harnesses. Then he saw something else. It was a blue kerchief waving in the wind. It had been tied to a willow on the riverbank.

He climbed up the bank and walked through some willows. He found a small camp. That's where he discovered the bodies of Constables Kinney and Taylor. They were lying next to each other.

It seemed that Kinney had died first. His body was laid out with both hands folded neatly across his chest. Next to him was the twisted body of Taylor. Taylor had shot himself. The search party covered the men with branches. They continued on down the Peel River. They hoped that Fitzgerald and Carter were alive.

They travelled 16 kilometres farther down the river. They found a faint trail that went up to the riverbank. They followed it. A pair of snowshoes was found. Then, they saw the bodies of Fitzgerald and Carter. Fitzgerald had died after Carter. It looked like he had dragged Carter's body three metres from their campfire. He had crossed Carter's arms over his body and placed a handkerchief over his face. Fitzgerald's body was found lying beside the campfire. He had two thin blankets pulled around him. They were only 40 kilometres from Fort McPherson.

The search party covered the men's bodies with branches. Then they raced to Fort McPherson with the tragic news. A few days later, the bodies were brought back to Fort McPherson for burial. They received full military honours in the churchyard of the Church of England mission.

Continuing the Road to Nowhere
In 1904 King Edward VII added "Royal" to the name of the NWMP. The new name was Royal North-West Mounted Police (RNWMP). The name changed again in

1920 to Royal Canadian Mounted Police (RCMP).

In 1897, the Canadian government had given Inspector Moodie the order to build an all-Canadian road to the Yukon. Eight years later, in 1905, the government gave a similar order. It demanded the RNWMP build a pack trail from Peace River to the Yukon.

Why the government wanted the Yukon trail project reopened in 1905 is not clear. The gold rush was over. The population in the North was not large. Perhaps the government was worried that the Americans would claim the Yukon as their own. Whatever the reason, the Mounties had to carry out the orders.

The RNWMP were told to build a trail for pack ponies. Later it needed to be widened for a wagon trail. The route chosen would be based on the one first suggested by Moodie after his 1897–1898 survey patrol. The Mounties had to construct the road. They also had to build bridges. Every 48 kilometres they had to build rest houses for future travellers and put up mileposts.

Leading the expedition was Superintendent Charles Constantine. With him went Inspector Richard, 30 officers and constables, and 60 horses. They were to build a 2.6-metre-wide trail stretching 1200 kilometres. It would run from Fort St. John to Teslin in the Yukon. Constantine was told, "the work must be rushed."

The party arrived at Fort St. John on June 1. They spent the first two weeks there. They constructed a small police barrack for their summer and winter quarters.

On June 15, the men began building the Peace River–Yukon trail. They built bridges across streams and levelled steep banks. They hacked through trees and bushes. They climbed over mountain passes. They hiked down into valleys through swampy lowlands. It was hard and tiring work.

Just over three months later, they had finished building 150 kilometres of highway and were getting ready for winter.

It was a bitterly cold first winter for the men at Fort St. John. Their supply ship had been unable to get supplies to them. So the Mounties were forced to drive one-horse sleighs over the difficult mountain trails. The burden was so hard for the horses that they had to be helped to stand each morning. The men had no new clothing. Some wore moose hides and flour sacks in place of their tattered clothes.

By August 1906, another 215 kilometres of trail had been built. The pack route now reached Fort Grahame, 320 kilometres from Fort St. John. The conditions had been terrible. Thirteen horses had died. Then the exhausted men had to build a small barracks at Fort Grahame for winter quarters. They even had to build horse corrals.

By spring 1907, the men were once again building their road. By September 1907, they had added another 241 kilometres to the trail. Now a total of 575 kilometres had been built. That autumn, Commissioner Perry inspected the trail. He declared it was a good one.

The end of building the road was now in sight. After three seasons of exhausting work, the all-Canadian backdoor route to the Yukon would soon be opened.

Then the federal government gave an order to Commissioner Perry. Perry was told to ask the British Columbia government to help pay for the new road. The BC government refused to share the costs. So the federal government decided to stop further building of the road.

The Mounties were disappointed. The 575 kilometres of the Peace River–Yukon trail had taken three years of their lives to build. Now it became an abandoned road to nowhere.

One Last Effort

In 1910, a third road-building patrol was assigned to the Road to Nowhere. This time, 34-year-old Sergeant John "Jock" Darling would lead the trail builders. The road would continue to Whitehorse through Telegraph Creek and Atlin.

The men left Athabasca Landing on May 4, 1910. They took with them saddle horses, wagon teams, and 11 packhorses. Problems began right away. A wagon turned over twice and had to be reloaded. After that, it was just one hardship after another.

The group had to deal with bush fires. Their horses caused them problems. The wagon teams couldn't keep up with the packhorses. The trails were brutal and injured their horses. Then there was the weather. Snow, rain, and thunderstorms made life difficult. They rescued wagons stuck in muskeg. They had to build bridges across swollen rivers. And the mosquitoes and black flies drove them crazy.

On June 5, they arrived at Lake St. John in British Columbia. They had been gone a month. The next 950 kilometres were very hard. This time it was deep, snow-covered valleys and high mountains that challenged them. Trails were blocked by snow and bridges were rotten. Sometimes the horses stampeded.

One of the hardest days of the expedition was June 23. The party had to cross the Osipaka River in the rain. At 5 a.m., the men started to build a raft. It had to be large enough to take wagons and supplies across the river. They used too much heavy timber and had to rebuild it. It took eight trips to get the equipment across the river. The men had to swim the horses across.

When they arrived at Atlin on October 5, they still had 200 kilometres to go. The group decided they'd had enough of trekking through bush. Instead, they hopped on the steamer *Atlin*. They finally landed in Whitehorse. During the five-month trek, the Darling Patrol had covered 2700 kilometres.

Three times the Mounties had faced great challenges while trying to build a trail to the Yukon. Three times, the wilderness won. The Road to Nowhere was never finished.

Chapter 5
Crazy Exploits in North Country

Living in the far North is difficult. You can get lonely. You can go all winter without seeing much sunlight. Some people feel depressed. Old timers call it "cabin fever." It can push even the strongest man crazy. Some men became so bothered that they kill themselves or others.

Sometimes people with cabin fever needed to get to the hospital. The Mounties took people from their home to the hospital. They called this the "Lunatic Patrol." In one year alone, more than 40 such patrols were made between Dawson City and Whitehorse.

Sergeant Field was stationed at Fort Chipewyan in 1902. A message came. A man had gone "violently insane" in Hay River, 560 kilometres north of Fort Chipewyan. The only way to get to Hay River was by dog team. Field hooked up his dogs and set off with a Native interpreter. Field knew that if the man had gone insane, he would have to bring him out by dogsled.

Field hoped the man's illness would be mild enough that it could be treated at Fort Chipewyan. But, if the man's illness was severe, a difficult journey lay ahead for both the Mountie and the sick man.

When Field got to Hay River, things didn't look good. The man was snarling like a wild animal. He had a wicked glare for anyone who came near him. Field had no choice but to take him to the hospital. It would be a 1600-kilometre journey to Fort Saskatchewan.

For the next six weeks, Sergeant Field protected and cared for this man. He fed and exercised him. He guarded him. He protected him from frostbite in the freezing temperatures and blinding blizzards. And he slept beside him.

Field was careful to keep weapons out of the man's reach. By day, Field listened to the man's mad ravings. At night he listened to his screams.

Once Field reached Fort Saskatchewan, medical authorities took over. His job was done. Field turned around and headed back to his regular duties at Fort Chipewyan.

Sometimes it was stressful being on Lunatic Patrol. Even the strongest Mounties could break down, like Constable Albert Pedley. He was also stationed at Fort Chipewyan.

British-born Pedley was 22 years old when he joined the NWMP on April 18, 1900. After spending three months in Regina, he was stationed at Fort Saskatchewan. Then he moved to Fort Chipewyan.

Pedley's Lunatic Patrol began on December 17, 1904. He and an interpreter, Special Constable Damies, left Fort Chipewyan with two dog teams. They had to bring a mentally ill missionary to a hospital in Fort Saskatchewan, 800 kilometres away. Pedley put the man in a sleeping bag. He then covered him in thick fur and strapped him onto the police dogsled. For the next five days, Pedley and the interpreter ran behind the sleds. There was slush and water up to their knees. It was brutal and demanding.

The temperature was bitterly cold. At Fort McKay, Pedley bought moccasins for the missionary's frozen feet. The weather continued to worsen. The temperature plunged to –50 degrees Celsius. A blizzard swept in. It became too dangerous to continue. To protect the dogs, Pedley dug them a trench. He used the overturned sled as their windbreak.

The missionary stayed in the sleeping bag. But Pedley and the interpreter tied him to a tree so that the strong winds would not blow him away. Then they climbed into their own sleeping bags. The also tied themselves to the trees.

The storm lasted for 48 hours. Once it was over, the group left. They headed south to wooded country.

It was more sheltered. It was also full of timber wolves. Each evening, Pedley lit a huge fire. This helped protect themselves from the hungry wolves. They kept the fire going all night.

The sick missionary wouldn't eat at times. And he tried to escape twice. The second time, he waited until Pedley's arms were full of wood. Then he bolted to freedom. Pedley chased him through the snow for almost a kilometre. Finally he caught him. He tied his hands and feet. He carried the man back to the camp through a bitter wind.

The patrol arrived at Lac La Biche on New Year's Eve. They were in time for some celebrating. Special Constable Damies attended a dance. At 10 p.m., he raced back to get Pedley. A fight had broken out.

The Mountie arrived on the scene. He quickly arrested a drunken troublemaker. Then he looked for the rest of the liquor. He searched two houses in the community. He found brandy and whisky. He arrested two more men.

Now he had the missionary and three drunks in his custody. Before they could continue, another sled and dog team had to be hired. The group finally left Lac La Biche on January 2. They headed for Fort Saskatchewan.

Two days later, the group arrived at Saddle Lake. Pedley explained the situation before a justice of the peace. The next day, the three men were convicted.

Pedley continued on to Fort Saskatchewan with Special Constable Damies and the missionary.

The exhausted RNWMP patrol arrived in Fort Saskatchewan on January 7, 1905. The missionary needed a hospital. His feet were badly frozen. So was his tongue. The nearest hospital was in Calgary. Less than two months later, the missionary was able to leave the hospital. He had lost part of his big toe. But his mind and speech were back to normal.

Things didn't go as well for Pedley. Before leaving Fort Saskatchewan, Pedley travelled to Edmonton to see a dentist. He left in good health, but in Lac La Biche, he went violently insane. The hardships of the trip and his worry for the safety of the missionary had been too much for him.

The others had noticed that his health was not good. Pedley didn't eat or sleep for five days. On February 13, he became violently ill. His got even sicker. He had to return to Fort Saskatchewan.

Pedley was moved to a hospital in Brandon, Manitoba. He stayed there until October 4. Then three months later, Pedley returned to his job as a Mountie. Soon he was promoted to corporal and sergeant. He retired in 1924. Everyone talked about what happened to him. Later his experiences became the basis for a 1952 Hollywood movie. The movie was called *The Wild North*.

Peace River Sleuth

The North was large. Very few people lived there. A crime could go unnoticed. In 1904, a Utah trader by the name of Charles King almost got away with murder. But thanks to the detective work of a dog, a young Native boy, and a Mountie named Kristjan Fjeldsted "Andy" Anderson, he did not.

Born in Iceland in 1866, Anderson moved to Canada in 1887. He worked on the railway at first. Then he joined the NWMP in Regina on August 19, 1889. He spent most of his career in the North. He served in Maple Creek, Fort Saskatchewan, Lesser Slave Lake, and Grouard.

Anderson was a big man. He was also powerful. He had a hard-featured face. His eyes were piercing and blue. People noticed him. They also noticed his hard work and his courage. He became a bit of a northern legend. Old timers said that Anderson was "the toughest policeman they had ever known."

In August 1904, Staff Sergeant Anderson was posted at Lesser Slave Lake. Utah trapper Charles King and a rich British man named Edward Hayward left Edmonton for Peace River Country. They'd be gone for a year of trapping and hunting.

The pair travelled over the Swan Hills Trail to Lesser Slave Lake. On September 17, the men camped on the reserve at Sucker Creek. They spent time with the Sucker Creek peoples. The next day, King closed up camp alone. He left. He said that Hayward had already gone on to Sturgeon Lake.

Chief Moos Toos of the Sucker Creek people did not believe him. He and others had heard a gunshot the night before. Someone had also seen King build a big fire.

A few days later, Moos Toos told Staff Sergeant Anderson that two white men had camped on the Sucker Creek reserve. Two had come, but only one had left.

After King had left, the women went to see if anything useful had been left behind. They noticed how large the campfire had been. One of the women looked above the fire and noticed layers of fat on some tree leaves. This woman told Moos Toos, "Someone burned flesh at that fire."

Also, a young Native boy noticed that the trappers' dog had refused to follow King when he left. He stayed close to the campsite instead.

Something was wrong, said Moos Toos. Staff Sergeant Anderson and Constable Lowe agreed. All three men went to the campsite. Raking the ashes, they found buttons and bone fragments. Then, in a hole under the ashes, they discovered bits of flesh and what looked like a human heart.

Nearby, Moos Toos and his people waded barefoot in the slough. On the muddy bottom they found a camp kettle. They also found a pair of boots.

Anderson and Lowe rode after King and arrested him. Anderson returned to the campfire site to look for more evidence. He sifted through the ashes once again. He hired the Native peoples to dig a ditch to drain the slough.

The slough held several valuable clues: buttons, a belt buckle, a pocketknife, and bones. The bones were later identified as spinal vertebrae. A bullet was rooted in them. The bullet was the same kind that King's revolver used.

Also, there was a money case. It had the name of an English company engraved on it. Anderson traced the case back to England. He discovered that Hayward's father had purchased the case for his son to take with him to northern Canada. The clues were neatly falling into place — even though there was no body.

Charles King was tried for murder in Edmonton in February 1905. No body was ever found, but there was lots of evidence. King was found guilty. He was put to death on September 30, 1905, at Fort Saskatchewan.

Head in a Sack

Mounties sometimes had to be creative. One of the strangest tales is of Staff Sergeant Andy Anderson. Anderson once carried a human head from the Peace River area to a courtroom in Kamloops.

The story began in 1910. Two trappers named Coleman and Trotter had a fight one day. The men had been living together for the winter season at Coleman Creek. As the tale goes, Coleman became angry with Trotter. Trotter was hollowing out a log with a hammer and chisel. He was making a water trough.

Some say Coleman may have had cabin fever. He suddenly reached for his gun. It had been hanging on the wall. Trotter saw Coleman reach for his weapon. He slammed his partner's head hard with the hammer. This caused Coleman to fall into the roaring fire in the cabin's fireplace. His body was burned.

Terrified, Trotter ran for help from a storeowner. Storeowner Tremblay was about 16 kilometres away. The men returned. Coleman was dead. Without moving Coleman's body, Tremblay left Trotter in charge of his store. Tremblay sped by dog team over 250 kilometres. He reported the death to Anderson and the RNWMP detachment at Peace River.

Once back at Coleman Creek, Anderson checked the murder site. He arrested Trotter for the killing. He then had to bring both men back to Kamloops for the murder trial. The dead body was now frozen stiff.

At the trial, Trotter would be charged with murder or self-defence. The dead body was the piece of evidence. Really, the head was the only part of the dead body that had any evidence on it. Anderson had an idea.

The Mountie chopped off the head and put it in a pail. Then he put the pail in a gunnysack. He tied the sack up and left.

In the evenings, to prevent animals from getting at the head, Anderson had to hang the gunnysack high in the trees. One night he almost lost the head. He hung the bag a little too low and the sled dogs pulled it down. They were just about to destroy the evidence. Trotter woke Anderson up in time to rescue the head.

Later on their trip, the officer and his prisoner battled a terrible snowstorm. Both were very tired. Anderson wanted to rest. Trotter insisted they keep going or they would freeze to death. Trotter saved Anderson's life by keeping him moving until the blizzard was over.

At the Kamloops trial, Anderson showed the severed head as evidence. It didn't make a strong case for murder. Anderson asked the judge what he thought the cause of death was.

The judge replied, "Decapitation, of course!"

Trotter told the judge and jury that he killed Coleman in self-defence. He was found not guilty. When the trial ended, Anderson and Trotter headed back together to Peace River Country.

After a colourful career, Anderson retired from the RCMP on January 1, 1921. He died in January 1949. The force had lost another great Mountie.

Chapter 6
Rescuing a Wizard

I n 1902, the border between the Yukon and Alaska was still being argued over. It was said that the Americans were ready to invade and take the Yukon from Canada. Senior police and government officials took the threats seriously. Superintendent Constantine returned to the Yukon. He developed a plan. He made lists of available military personnel in the territory. He ordered two machine guns.

It was a tense time. The NWMP were careful not to start anything. They just waited. But on February 1, 1902, something very strange happened to three NWMP constables.

It was nighttime. An excited missionary stormed into the NWMP post at Wells. He had come from the village of Kluk-wan, a few kilometres away in Alaska.

The officer in charge was Constable A. G. Leeson. He listened carefully. The missionary, Mr. Sellon, told of a young Chilcat boy being tortured. The band's elders had accused him of doing witchcraft.

The missionary begged for help. He said that the boy, named Kodik, would soon die. But Leeson couldn't just rush over to Alaska to save the boy. He was a Canadian police officer. He had no authority in the United States.

Still he wanted to do something. He could not go over as a police officer. But he could cross the border as a citizen carrying his own pistol. That's what he could do to save the boy.

Two other constables volunteered to join him. Quickly, they changed into regular clothes. They packed their own revolvers and a pick, a shovel, and an axe. They crossed into American territory.

Mr. Sellon led them to an empty house in the village. The boy was not there. They were about to leave. Then one of the officers noticed a woodpile on the outer porch. It looked odd. He moved the firewood. He lifted two loose floor planks underneath. There he found an ice-coated hole. In the hole was a boy curled up. It was very cold outside. It was around −40 degrees Celsius.

The men wrapped the boy in blankets. They carried him to the missionary's house. Once Kodik was warm, he had a bit of food. Then he told them a horrible story. To lessen his "evil" powers, the elders had kicked his head. Then they had starved him. Then they beat him. Then they jabbed his chest with sharp-pointed sticks. After, they had tied his hands behind his back. Then they scalded him with steam from a boiling kettle. Finally, they threw him into the icy hole in the porch. He was left to freeze to death.

Soon angry Chilcat elders surrounded the mission. They demanded the return of Kodik, the "wizard." One of the chiefs, Yiltock, also wanted to kill Mr. Sellon. But he stopped. He recognized the man standing beside the missionary with his gun drawn. It was the out-of-uniform Canadian Mountie, Constable Leeson. Yiltock explained to Leeson that witchcraft was killing his people. They needed to stop it. He needed Kodik returned to him. Leeson refused.

The Chilcat surrounded the house all night. At dawn they disappeared. Most of the people in the village were sleeping. Quickly, the officers bundled up the boy. They smuggled him past the village and across the border. He was safe in their police detachment. Kodik stayed until he got a safe spot in the Alaska Industrial School at Sitka.

Mounties in Siberia

In May 1919, six RNWMP officers and 154 horses were in eastern Siberia. They were about to travel 6000 kilometres across war-torn Russia by train. This would be one of the most unusual episodes in Mountie history.

World War I was over. Russia was in the middle of a civil war between its new Soviet government and the White Russians. The new government had gained power after the Bolshevik Revolution in October 1917. The White Russians were anti-Bolshevik. They were trying to get control again.

On August 12, 1918, Canada formed a force to help the White Russians. This included a Mountie cavalry unit. It was known as Squadron B. It had 190 men and 181 police horses. The well-trained horses were from ranches in Alberta and Saskatchewan. Many had served with the Mounties for years.

A 20-man RNWMP party sailed first to Vladivostok. They left in early October. The rest of the men, plus the horses, left Vancouver on November 17. Before the second group even set sail, the war in Europe had come to an end. The Armistice had been signed on November 11. The squadron left anyway.

The eastern Siberia port city of Vladivostok was full of Allied troops. Their job was to stop the region from falling to the Bolsheviks. They also had to keep the Trans-Siberian Railroad open.

The Mounties didn't see any action in Siberia. In April 1919, the Canadian forces began to leave Siberia. The men were happy to go home. But the Mountie horses of Squadron B would not be returning with them. Instead, they were to be delivered to the White Russians fighting at Yekaterinburg in the Ural Mountains. This meant the animals would have to go on a long and dangerous train journey of 6400 kilometres.

Six Mounties volunteered to travel with the horses. The rest of Squadron B prepared to sail back to Canada.

Sergeant J. E. "Teddy" Margetts was in charge of the volunteer Mounties who travelled with the horses. As they moved toward Yekaterinburg through northern China, many stops were made. The horses needed fresh water and exercise. Even so, some of the horses became ill.

Two weeks later, the Bolsheviks attacked the train. The train was derailed on a steep hill. Boxcars were overturned. Nineteen of them were "smashed to atoms." Twenty-four Russian soldiers were injured. Two Russian guards and 15 horses died.

The scene was a disaster. Many horses were trapped inside the overturned boxcars. Others lay in the wreckage. Some were so badly injured that they had to be destroyed. Sergeant Margetts quickly took charge of the rescue operation. His actions allowed the trapped animals to be rescued.

In the confusion, 20 to 30 horses ran away. Four Mounties — led by Corporal Philip Bossard — quickly went after the fleeing horses. They risked getting shot at or captured. They wanted to bring every horse back to the train. They did.

Several days later, the train was moving again. It arrived at Yekaterinburg on June 25, 1919. The Mounties handed the horses over to the White Russians. Then they headed back to Vladivostok and took a steamer home to Canada.

A few days after the horses arrived, the White Russians left and the city was captured by the Bolsheviks. In October of 1919, the Russian civil war was over. The new Soviet Bolshevik government was firmly in power. No one knows what happened to the horses.

Both Margetts and Brossard were recognized for their leadership during the train attack. Margetts received the Meritorious Service Medal. Bossard received the Military Medal for "Gallantry and Distinguished Service."

Salt Water Cowboys

Sometimes the Mounties had to patrol the waters. Those Mounties who patrolled the waters called themselves "saltwater cowboys and horse marines."

By the 1920s, it was illegal to sell or drink alcohol. On the Canadian east coast, liquor was being sold. Many people were involved with rumrunning. Some of the best captains were thought to be rumrunners. The RCMP went in to stop this. The RCMP was kept busy. In one year, they carried out more than 400 rumrunning patrols.

One night, July 3, Detective-Sergeant J. P. Blakeney, Corporal W. A. Caldwell, and Constable F. P. Fahey dressed in plain clothes. They set out to sea in a motorboat in search of the boat *Veda M. McKeown*. This was a known rumrunner boat. They soon sighted the schooner. It was anchored and waiting for buyers to come and purchase liquor.

The RCMP steered the police boat alongside the schooner. Pretending to be a buyer, Blakeney climbed aboard the ship. He argued with the captain over the price of whisky, rum, and gin. They finally agreed to a price. Blakeney watched the liquor being passed to the RCMP boat. Just before the last of the liquor was given over, the captain stopped. He wanted the money paid first.

Blakeney introduced himself as a sergeant of the Royal Canadian Mounted Police. He arrested the rumrunners. While he was talking, his partners, Caldwell and Fahie, jumped on board.

This caught the rumrunners by surprise. Everyone was quiet. Finally, the captain and crew surrendered. They were later prosecuted. The liquor was brought ashore.

Even 40 years after their first liquor arrest in 1873, the Mounties stopped the activities of the illegal liquor trade.

Medical Emergency

In 1923, Constable Stallworthy was stationed north at the Chesterfield Inlet detachment. A year later, he was joined by Staff Sergeant S. G. Clay and his 33-year-old wife Margaret. "Maggie" was one of the few white women in the Arctic. This was not Maggie's first time in the North. She had lived in the Mackenzie River area.

Shortly after they arrived at Chesterfield Inlet, Staff Sergeant Clay was invited to join the HBC traders. They were leaving on their fall patrol up the Back River to Baker Lake. Maggie encouraged her husband to go. He should get to know the area. He should meet some of the Native peoples. She was used to spending many hours alone. Besides, she was happy to stay and learn about her new community.

Maggie liked to walk along the beach. Children often played there. It was a September afternoon when Constable Stallworthy heard a dogfight on the beach. Then he heard Maggie scream. Corporal O. G. Petty also heard the scream.

Both men rushed out of their post. They were greeted by a horrible scene. Maggie was lying on the ground. Surrounding her were snarling dogs. They had ripped the flesh from her knee to her ankle. Bare bone was exposed. The men chased the dogs away. They picked Maggie up carefully. She was carried to her home.

Stallworthy worked with two HBC men and two Roman Catholic priests. They stopped the blood loss. They tried to make Maggie comfortable. Maggie was in terrible pain. She begged the men to cut off her leg. Feeling they had no choice but to amputate, the men agreed that they would.

Father Duplesne would perform the surgery. The

HBC's trading post manager, Norman Snow, would assist him. Petty and Stallworthy would look after the surgical instruments and dressing. During the surgery, Stallworthy would give the anaesthetic.

None of the men had done this kind of medical procedure before. They had only basic surgical tools and supplies. The men spent the night studying the one medical book they had.

There was no such thing as antibiotics then. There was a risk of infection. Everyone, including Maggie, signed a pre-surgery statement: "We believe that the amputation of Mrs. Clay's leg is necessary. We have every reason to believe that we can succeed. We believe that this will save her life."

The dining room table became the operating table. Stallworthy gave Maggie the chloroform. When it had taken effect, Father Duplesne began the surgery. When it came time for the priest to saw through the bone, he couldn't do it. Constable Stallworthy quickly took over. He finished amputating the leg just as the effects of the chloroform wore off.

Awake when Stallworthy carried her to her bed, Maggie asked, "Is my leg off? I feel so much better." A little later she asked, "I won't be able to dance again, will I?"

At first, everyone was hopeful that Maggie would recover. However, the shock and blood loss was too great. She became worse.

Maggie knew she was dying. She would never see

her husband again. She had Stallworthy write down her thoughts and messages to her husband. The constable comforted her and gave her sips of tea. About midnight of the third day, she died.

The men made her a simple coffin. Then, after an Anglican memorial service, Maggie was buried on the hill behind the detachment.

A few weeks later, her husband returned. Stallworthy met him. He knew something was wrong immediately. He shouted, "Where is Maggie?" Stallworthy told him. He was devastated.

The following spring, both Stallworthy and Clay left Chesterfield Inlet. They went to tell Maggie's family of her death. Clay left the Force.

Stallworthy visited England. Then he moved to the Jasper detachment. Later he was stationed at Bache Peninsula on Ellesmere Island. He became one of Canada's greatest Arctic travellers.

The Incredible Sea Saga of the *St. Roch*
Throughout the 1920s, the RCMP continued to push northern boundaries. They built police posts throughout the Yukon, the Northwest Territories, and the Arctic Archipelago. In 1927, the Force decided to get its own patrol ship for the Arctic.

A small schooner named *St. Roch* was built to do the job. By the time it was retired 26 years later, the *St. Roch* had become a seafaring legend. So had its captain, Staff Sergeant Henry A. Larsen.

In 1903, there were more than 400 years of failed attempts by sailors and ships to get through the Northwest Passage. Then Norwegian explorer Roald Admunsen tried with his small ship *Gjoa*. He was successful. It took the explorer three years (1903–1906) to journey from the Atlantic Ocean, across the top of North America, to the Pacific Ocean.

It would be many more years before a ship vessel would sail the passage from west to east. Or travel it both ways. But then it did happen. In 1940, the RCMP and their boat, *St. Roch*, were sent on a secret wartime mission. They made seafaring history.

The *St. Roch* was built in Vancouver during the winter of 1927–1928. She was 32 metres long with an 8-metre beam. Her engine was a 150 horsepower Union Diesel engine. Douglas fir and Australian gumwood were the woods used. They were the only wood known to withstand the grinding effects of ice pressure.

She was small and not a very pretty ship. Larsen called her "Ugly Duckling."

From 1928 to 1940, the *St. Roch* travelled the western Arctic waters from Vancouver to the Mackenzie River. Her winters were often spent frozen in the ice.

By the spring of 1940, the World War II was underway. All RCMP boats, like other Canadian ships, were put to work. Larsen was just getting ready to leave Vancouver in June for his annual winter patrol. He received a rather strange order. He was to set out for Greenland. It was a secret mission.

Larsen knew it would be a difficult trip. The little ship first had to sail east through the dangerous waters of the Northwest Passage. But if anyone could do it, it was Larsen. He was Canada's most experienced Arctic navigator and an expert on Arctic expeditions.

Born in Fredrikstad, Norway, in 1899, Larsen had been at sea since the age of 15. He had joined the RCMP in 1928. He began as the first mate aboard the newly launched *St. Roch*. By the end of that year, he had been become the skipper. For the next 20 years, he had taken the *St. Roch* on its annual Arctic patrols.

Larsen admired the Inuit for their ability to survive in a cold environment. He was sensitive to their culture. They taught him to handle a dog team and hunt seal. They called him *Hanorie Umiarjuag* (or *Umiarpolik*). It meant "Henry with the Big Ship."

On June 21, 1940, the *St. Roch* left Vancouver. From the beginning, things did not go smoothly. A few days after setting sail, engine trouble forced them to stop. They made repairs. Two weeks later, the ship entered the Bering Sea. The *St. Roch* ran into violent winds and rain. Both lasted all day and night. When the wind stopped, the ship continued.

On July 22, they saw just a bit of sea ice. Soon there was more. It got thicker and thicker. On July 24, they were forced to cut the engines. The *St. Roch* had to drift with the ice pack. By August 2, she was working eastward, mooring to ice floes when the ice got too heavy. Five days later, they were within sight of the Cross Islands. But the *St. Roch* was sandwiched in the floes. She was unable to move.

After 70 days at sea, the *St. Roch* arrived at Herschel Island. It was August 11. A month later, on September 16, the crew reached Cambridge Bay. They took on dogs for their winter patrols. It had been a rough journey.

Larsen had not planned to overwinter on this voyage. They were expected in Greenland. But the weather worked against them. It was now too late to try to complete the journey. The *St. Roch* would have to winter in the frozen ice. They sailed over to Walker Bay. It was on the west coast of Victoria Island.

The *St. Roch* arrived safely at the bay on October 5. They chose a wintering site about 270 metres from shore. Quickly, the crew unloaded the fuel oil, coal, and boats onto the beach. Before the bay was frozen on October 30, the *St. Roch* was covered in its winter home under a canvas-covered wooden frame.

The crew settled in for the long, dark winter. They still had to work. Work included dogsled patrolling. They watched the actions of foreign hunters and whalers. They visited the Inuit camps. They recorded weather, enforced game laws, and more.

For 10 months, the *St. Roch* remained frozen in the

ice at Walker Bay. It wasn't until July 31, 1941, that she sailed out of her winter quarters. They stopped quickly at Holman Island. There was a report of an accidental shooting of an Inuit boy. After, the ship ran into heavy scattered ice and thick wet fog. She inched along, stopping and mooring to ice floes to avoid danger.

On August 2, she anchored off Cape Bathhurst in deep fog. Later, she faced more fierce wind. The wind howled for days.

For the next month, the *St. Roch* encountered extreme weather conditions. Sometimes she had to take shelter for days at a time. Larsen continued to sail eastward. Sometimes the wind tossed and rolled the boat "like a cork."

The waters were frozen. There was no escape for the *St. Roch*. She had to winter again. This time she stayed at Pasley Bay.

A long and busy season lay ahead. A 61-day patrol was done. They needed to count how many Inuit lived in the area. The men travelled more than 1700 kilometres. It was never warmer than –48 degrees Celsius.

On August 3, 1942, after 11 months at Pasley Bay, the *St. Roch* left. Soon she met more ice that blocked the entrance to the bay. Larsen decided to see if the ice would break. It didn't. The *St. Roch* was again a prisoner of the ice.

It was a scary wait. At times, the ice pressure lifted the ship up as high as one metre. It caused her to rock from side to side. Back and forth, like "an egg-shell in a giant's playground" she drifted. It was very dangerous.

Several times, even Larsen felt they were doomed. Adding to their problems, part of their engine broke.

On August 24, the waters opened up. Slowly the ship made her way through the passage. Larsen worked the tide, dodging icebergs. He battled strong currents and jammed ice.

On September 6, the *St. Roch* arrived at Pond Inlet. They took on some fuel and then sailed into the Davis Strait. There was more ice, wind, and waves. But Larsen pushed through. They sailed past Baffin Island and down the coast of Labrador.

On September 30, the *St. Roch* reached Corner Brook, Newfoundland. On October 8, she reached Sydney Harbour, Cape Breton Island. And on October 11, at 3:30 p.m., after having travelled more than 15,000 kilometres and spending 819 days at sea, the little RCMP patrol boat arrived at Halifax.

The secret mission was never met. But the *St. Roch* became the second ship to successfully navigate the Northwest Passage. It was the first to sail from west to east.

In 1944, the *St. Roch* and Larsen once again sailed the passage. This time, they sailed from east to west. They completed the journey in three months (July 16 to October 16). This made history. The *St. Roch* was the first ship to navigate the passage both ways.

But she wasn't finished making history. In the early 1950s, she became the first ship to circle North America twice. When she returned to Vancouver in 1954, the city purchased the *St. Roch*. They towed her to Kits Point and brought her ashore. In 1962, the *St. Roch* was declared a National Historic Site. It is now on display at the Vancouver Maritime Museum.

Larsen left the *St. Roch* before 1950. He stayed with the RCMP as a superintendent. He retired in 1961 with 33 years of service. Larsen Sound (between James Ross Strait and Franklin Strait) and Larsen Inlet are named for him.

Epilogue

In the RNWMP Corps History of 1906, Captain Ernest J. Chambers wrote about a young constable. He had become lost on patrol during a severe winter blizzard. Before he died, the young Mountie had written down his thoughts.

"Lost, horse dead. Am trying to push ahead. Have done my best."

The words summed up the honour and sense of duty many of the RNWMP felt. That honour and sense of duty are still fitting for the women and men of today's RCMP. The spirit of honour, duty, and daring live on.